What Angela Needs

Written by Rita Benson
Illustrated by Linda McClelland

The morning after Angela's new baby brother arrived home, Angela's mother found her right at the foot of the bed, with the blankets over her head.

"I had a bad dream," Angela sobbed.

So that night, Mum tucked Bernard, Angela's toy tiger, next to her in bed.

"There you are," said Mum. "Bernard will look after you. Give him a big hug if you wake up in the night."

But, in the middle of the night, when Angela put out her hand for a cuddle, Bernard was gone. Mum found him under the bed.

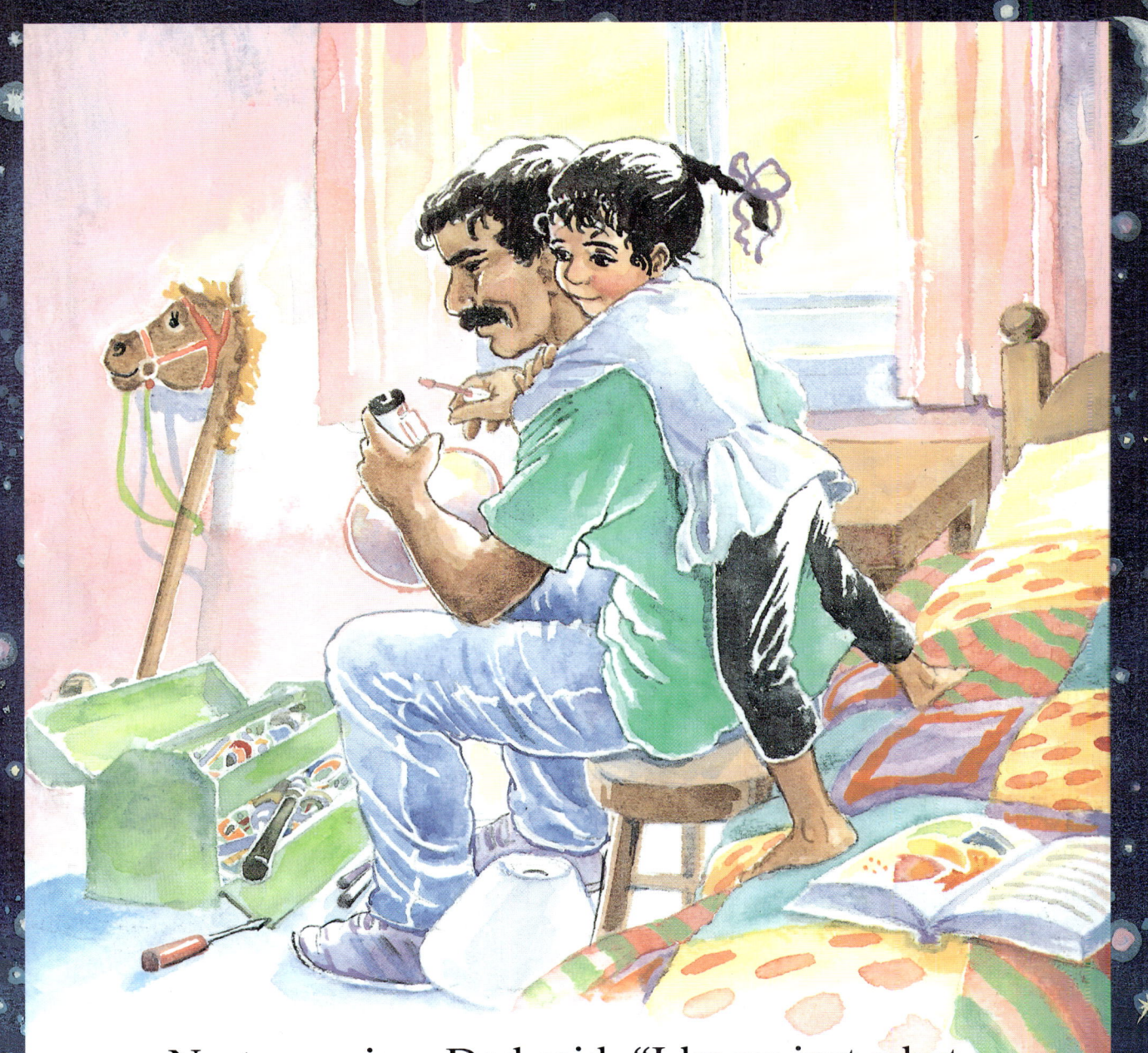

Next morning, Dad said, "I know just what to do." He got out his screwdriver and put a special switch on the light in Angela's room.

"Now we can leave the light on low for you during the night," he said.

But, in the middle of the night, the shadows became monsters. They stood on Angela's furniture, and wore her clothes.

Mrs Loft, next door, put her head over the fence.

"What Angela needs," she said in a wise voice, "is a cup of nice warm milk before she goes to bed. Then she'll sleep soundly."

But, in the middle of the night, Angela needed to go to the bathroom, on her own, in the dark.

Later that week, Grandpa took Angela to the museum.

"You'll be so tired after our day out, Angela," he told her, "you'll sleep like a log."

But that night, Angela had a dream that she was lost and tired, and she couldn't find her way home.

"I think we will visit the doctor," said Mum, the next day. "He might have some good ideas."

"Well," said Dr MacNab, "perhaps what Angela needs is a security blanket."

When they got home, Mum found Angela's old blanket.

"You used to love this," she said. "You can take it to bed with you tonight."

But, during the night, the blanket got tangled up with the sheets, and Angela couldn't find it.

The next weekend, Uncle John came to visit. He lived on a dairy farm in the country. Angela loved the way he smelled of hay and cows. She rushed out to meet him.

"What have you got in the box, Uncle John?"

"Come and see," said Uncle John, with a smile. Together, they opened the box.

"Oh, it's a kitten!" Angela cried, picking up the tiny ball of fluff.

"I thought you might like a little friend, Angie," said Uncle John.

Angela played with the kitten all day and, that night, it snuggled up at her feet, on the bed.

But, during the night, the kitten walked on her bed, and Angela's cry brought Mum and Dad rushing to her room.

The next day, Mum said, "I think Baby David could share your room now. Will you help me move his things in, Angela?"

Angela helped Mum bring in David's cot. She even put some of her toys in it for him to play with.

That night, Angela didn't dream of anything. And she didn't even wake up when David cried to be fed.